The

Emergent

Self

Other Books by
Adrian van Kaam and Susan Muto

Aging Gracefully
Am I Living A Spiritual Life?
The Commandments: Ten Ways to a Happy Life and a Healthy Soul
Commitment: Key to Christian Maturity
Divine Guidance: Seeking to Find and Follow the Will of God
The Emergent Self
Epiphany Manual on the Art and Discipline of Formation-in-Common
Formation Guide To Becoming Spiritually Mature
Harnessing Stress: A Spiritual Quest
Healthy and Holy Under Stress: A Royal Road to Wise Living
The Participant Self
The Power of Appreciation: A New Approach to Personal and Relational
Healing
Practicing the Prayer of Presence
Readings from A to Z: The Poetry of Epiphany
Songs for Every Season
Stress and the Search for Happiness:
A New Challenge for Christian Spirituality
Tell Me Who I Am
The Woman's Guide to the Catechism of the Catholic Church

The Emergent Self

Adrian van Kaam
and
Susan Muto

Revised Edition

EPIPHANY
ASSOCIATION
Pittsburgh, Pennsylvania

Scripture selections are taken from the *New Revised Standard Version*. Catholic Edition. New York: Oxford University Press, 1999.

Published by

Epiphany Books
Pittsburgh, Pennsylvania 15216

©2001 by the Epiphany Association

Library of Congress 2001094483
ISBN 1-880982-20-X

Printed in the United States of America

Contents

Part Three: The Self and Community

Part Four: The Self and Reality

Acknowledgments

Each chapter of *The Emergent Self* flows from a question about the meaning of life in relation to the self, the self and others, the self and community, and the self and reality.

Our responses are the fruit of formative thinking, prayerful dialogue, and painstaking editorial precision.

This writing on life and living emerged in the light of our human and Christian experience. Some material in *Envoy*, a magazine we once published, provided inspiration for these chapters. However, the revision and execution of this edition of *The Emergent Self* are entirely original.

Aiding us in this task with accuracy and devotion have been our Epiphany staff and most notably our administrative secretary, Mary Lou Perez, to whom we express our immense gratitude.

We invite all who open these pages to join us in a spirit of meditative reading and reflection. Relaxed presence to and abiding with the text will benefit anyone seeking deeper insight into life's meaning.

—The Authors

Preface

When we suffer,
when we are alone,
in moments of joy and grateful
anticipation of good times to come,
when we rest and relax and peacefully
recollect
the manifold aspects of our lives —
in the forest,
at the shore,
before falling asleep,
how often do we go beyond
the cares of the moment
and drift silently into the ocean of thought
whose waves are never still.
We trip lightly into strange waters,
recede cautiously, hesitate briefly —
and then decide:
Yes, the risk is worth it.

We return to the text
and experience for ourselves
the world of thought
and meditation,
which opens before us.

Boundless are its treasures,
more numerous than we shall ever know.

8

The Bible.
The history of humanity.
The presence of the Divine.
Our part in the unfolding
of the universe.
Goodness. Mercy. Justice. Humility.
Love. Happiness. Death.

Like old friends
deepest thoughts emerge
when least expected —
in a line of poetry,
a fragment of prose,
a favorite prayer.
In silent contemplation,
mindful of meditation,
we participate,
however fleetingly,
in the accumulated wisdom
of humanity.

How blessed we are
that generations have not kept
these treasures
of thought and experience
to themselves!

From rudimentary cave drawings
to computerized equations,
we have shared
these disclosures
with others over the ages.

What is meaningful
to one person's innermost being
may be as meaningful
to another's.
Thus do we make
our private speculations
public,
our silence
speech.

How poor we would be
were we to keep secret
all that has been revealed to us
on this voyage of discovery!

Imagine
a world devoid of sensuous
experience,
a world without touch
or sight
or sound,
a world
in which no one read
or thought
or spoke.

No matter how prosaic,
no matter how poetic
these experiences may be,
the man or woman of thought and feeling
longs to convey them
in an understandable way
to others.

Part One

The Self

Prologue

To see the true self
is not attained
without fortitude,

not without discipline.

I.
Emergence of Self

*To become aware of who I am and to integrate this aware-
ness into my life as a whole seems to foster the emergence
of my true self. Does this process ever come to a standstill
or must it continue over a lifetime?*

⮑

Life is such that we never reach a stage beyond which we cannot emerge in some way. The emergence of self is a continuous
event. We never arrive. We are forever arriving.

Our formation as persons continues from birth to death. It is
necessary but not always easy to persevere. That is why it takes
courage to carry on and not come to a standstill.

It helps to receive encouragement from one another. Sadly, we
often fail to appreciate the depth of our need for a kind word, a
friendly nod, a pat on the back.

We withhold small kindnesses on the pretense that they may
engender too much vainglory. We forget that we ourselves blossom under the warmth of a sincere compliment.

Our uncertainty about self-emergence is so great, our anxiety
so deep, that even a simple smile makes us feel worthwhile.

Some of us may have experienced so little tenderness that even the slightest show of compassion touches us. We need to feel appreciated and understood by one another to arrive at the assurance that we can go forward without feeling afraid.

It is one thing to become aware of our limitations, another to be hampered by them in our emergence.

Too often we turn against those who criticize us instead of searching for the grain of truth in what they say. It is easy to accuse others of callousness when in fact they may have rendered us a service by making us face the roadblocks on our journey.

A shortcoming remains a shortcoming even if it is communicated in a sensitive way. We are unwise to throw away the precious pearl because it comes in an unsightly shell. In proper order we can integrate compliments and criticisms into the pattern of our progress.

We must try to venture forth despite our misgivings. It is time to dive into the stream of life, not simply wade near the shore waiting for someone to push us into the waves. When we do hit the water, a good swim does wonders for us. Flowing with the current thrills us for two reasons: we are swimming under our own steam and we are moving with the rhythms of a greater mystery.

Emergence of self implies
looking again, seeing again, listening again,
as we involve ourselves with what is
and allow it to touch us where we are.

For most of us, the best moments in life are those we spend with the people we love. In their company we find joy.

Certain experiences bring us to a more heightened awareness of self and others. These are the times when we become aware of who we *are* and who we *are not*. Though all moments of life can be rewarding in some way, not all have the significance of being formative events.

Self-emergence is not simply a matter of playing it safe, of draping ourselves in the clothing of standard customs considered to be virtuous, but of being willing to take the risks associated with faith, hope, and love.

Our growth toward maturity implies the frank acknowledgment of our feelings and thoughts, our hopes and dreams, our intuitions and ideas. What do they mean in connection with our calling?

This attitude of openness invites us to see our attitudes and actions in the light of who God intends us to be. Disclosures occur over a lifetime and only occasionally all at once.

When we refuse to take responsibility for our own actions, we shift the scene to an anonymous "they." We look beyond the situation for our norms of behavior–to what "they" would say or do.

We must try to assume another attitude. At any moment, life may call for a candid and courageous response. To submit simply to what others want or demand is to deny the truth of our own compelling story. Now is time to take up the diary of our own emergence and read it diligently.

II.
Love and Self-Appreciation

It seems safe to say that in an insecure world we are prone to evaluate ourselves more or less according to others' expectations of us. What happens if we fail to meet them? Can we still learn to love our limits?

∽

As children we depend on the love we receive from our parents. We may have trouble overcoming our sense of not being worthwhile persons if we imagine their affection to be lacking.

This interplay of loving and being loved begins in the family. It prepares us to initiate our own circle of care in marriage or community.

For believers, a deeper dimension reveals itself. This is God's unconditional love for us despite what others may feel or think about us.

To be loved as children and to become loving adults is not only a gift of God to us; it is also the basis of our ability to become self-appreciative and appreciative of others. This faith enkindles in turn our sense of being precious in his sight.

As our true self continues to unfold, we discover what it means to love without always receiving equal love in return. Adulation and indiscriminate shows of affection are false sources of appreciation anyway. Gentle admonition at appropriate moments may better reveal our true worth and awaken a more realistic appraisal of our call.

There are many ways in which we can show others that we genuinely care. Blessings and bonuses when it's not a birthday, flowers on no special occasion, a look that says more than a flood of words–all these express tenderness and thanks and prolong cherished moments of loving togetherness.

To become appreciative is to put the needs of other people before our own and not to judge them in advance.

Many people are caught between the longing and the fear to love. She waits for him to reveal himself, he waits for her, but each hesitates to take the initiative. They may wait for a lifetime. To claim that every expression of love must be returned in kind is a sign of immaturity.

When self-gratification becomes more important than expressing our gratitude, the essence of love, to be self-gift, is lost.

When appreciation is gratuitous, it becomes a reservoir of faith, hope, and charity. The resulting experience of being persons of worth, loved for our own sake, is cause enough for thanks.

III.
Self-Emergence and Identification

Can we identify with others and at the same time discover our own identity? Is identification an obstacle or an aid to self-emergence?

⌐⌐

One way to discover who we are is to identify with good role models. Values remain elusive as long as we do not see them lived by trusted others. Their commitment to virtuous living inspires us to be like them. Before we know it, we may find ourselves feeling and acting as they do.

When we identify with others in this way, it ought not to surprise us if we also discover where we differ.

*Identification serves emergence
on the condition that
we do not forget
who we are.*

It impedes emergence to identify blindly with the appealing demeanor someone else displays. We risk becoming a conglomeration of borrowed modes of life that are more alienating than affirmative.

The attempt to adjust what we think and feel to another's judgments can stifle self-emergence. Our own call moves from the center to the periphery of our concerns. We depend more on others' opinions and rely less on our own. Our capacity for candid self-appraisal weakens.

Any type of blind conformity can be seen as an escape from taking responsibility for our own life. Although the lives of others can be admirable and inspirational, we need to be faithful to our call.

Constantly pretending to be someone else, never being myself, represents a radical break from the possibility of wholeness. My life is like a grand buffet, offering its patrons a little bit of everything and not much of anything. In trying so hard to be someone else, I end up being no one at all. I sell to the highest bidder what is best in me with the result that I am neither myself nor the other. Identification is a preparation, not a substitute, for finding ourselves.

This process benefits from relationships with people who draw forth different facets of our human and Christian personhood. Enriching as any passing meeting may be, it can never fulfill our longing for lasting presence to the Infinite Mystery beyond all limitations, who alone can satisfy our heart's desire.

To search is not to stand still until we stand before the Almighty who gives every limited epiphany of our identity a deeper meaning and blesses our emergence.

IV.
Self-Emergence and Imitation

*Imitation is said to be the "highest form of praise,"
but what if it causes us to model our lives more on
external appearances than on inner convictions?*

ᔭ

Persons whom we admire exemplify a quality we want to incorporate into our journey. What we see in them beams a spotlight on where we want to go. The goal we reach will not necessarily be what they have attained. Still emulation enhances our pursuit of knowledge. It enriches our response to every situation, different as it may be.

To mature is to become aware of styles of living that are compatible with our personality. It is normal to feel a certain affinity for some and an aversion for others.

As soon as we begin to explore how rich life can be, some form of imitation is unavoidable. It can be a fruitful experience, provided it does not deteriorate into a copy cat mentality.

*True imitation begins when we allow
external appearances to lead us
to an understanding of the
inner attitudes from whence they emerged.*

Accompanying this movement from outer imitation to inner commitment is the silent question: Is what I mirror in tune with my deepest self? If it is, then how can I come to my own expression of the values I so admire in others?

Imitation of anyone has to be in tune with our own call and the situation in which we find ourselves. We should know whom we desire to emulate and our motives for doing so. In this way, imitation can offer us the best of both worlds: to live in appreciation of another person and to be more fully the self we are called by God to be.

The most noble ideal for Christians is to imitate Christ. It is to embody his attitudes in our actions.

A missionary may mirror his preaching style; a nurse, his care for the sick; a contemplative, his silent pauses for prayer. Such imitation does not hinder self-unfolding, nor does it blind us to our uniqueness.

Self-emergence does imply diminishment of the need to imitate indiscriminately the life style of another person. The deeper the commitment to our calling becomes, the more selective we can be in regard to the imitation of others.

Problems arise when the desire for emulation degenerates into unoriginal duplication. We try not so much to *be* like the persons we admire as to *look* like them in all things. A piece of glass may be cut and polished to look like a diamond, but it remains a piece of glass.

There are persons who by their very presence challenge us to be our real selves. They would never think of putting their own mold of life on us as if we were pieces of clay on whom they could sculpt any image they like.

Appeal is the opposite of imposition. It allows us to incarnate in our own way the virtues and values we witness in the lives of human beings worthy to be emulated. Whatever happens we must always try to remain faithful to the path set by our own divine life direction.

Fidelity allows us to admire others without feeling compelled to imitate in rote fashion their growth in Christian personhood. God gives us our own guidelines and for that we are most grateful.

V.
Role Playing and Self-Discovery

How can we be ourselves if we have been wearing a mask or playing a role to avoid the need for self-discovery?

ᔓ

Progress in life would come to a halt if people did not play a role once in a while. A doctor chooses his words carefully to calm a frightened patient. A wife with news of a sensitive nature to share with her husband and children waits for the right moment.

Role-playing is not bad provided we remember that we are more than the masks we wear to be diplomatic, to protect our privacy, to exercise our profession, or not to hurt unnecessarily the feelings of others.

We have an intrinsic value that transcends any task we perform, career we attain, or role we play.

Self-discovery begins with
a truthful look at
who I am
over and beyond what I do.

As I hold up this mirror and take a good look at myself, I may discover that all I see are numerous reflections and not the real me. I change faces to meet the faces I have to meet.

This donning of different masks depletes my inner resources. Perhaps I have become the roles I play. This awareness may signal that it is time to change.

"Thus you will know them by their fruits," says the Lord (Matthew 7:20). And so it is for me. The masks I wear pale in importance compared to the person behind them. My deepest "I" is internal not external. I recognize who I am when my mask comes off, even though my whole story remains a secret only God fully knows.

I may never be able to bring to light all that I am, but I can accept the social and cultural roles I have to play without losing myself in the process.

The more I personalize these roles, the more something of the real me will shine through. In other words, my roles reveal and at the same time conceal who I am. I have to become an artist whose ability to play roles remains original and innovative.

Once I see the necessity of letting the roles I play express the values I hold, I am less likely to live a false existence. The self I am will shine through everything I do. Life becomes an epiphany free from the pressure of conformity and an excessive fear of offending others.

Shedding false roles and discovering my true self are necessary steps in the movement from alienation to emergence.

VI.
Rules, Regulations, and Self-Realization

Since maturity seems to be a matter of being and becoming my true self, what part do rules and regulations play in the process?

✑

Ours is a natural longing for freedom and autonomy while being confronted continually by the limits of life. There is that in us which would like to be totally independent; yet wherever we turn we discover that we are dependent in some measure.

The language we speak is *our* language, the nationality we share is *our* nationality, the culture we enjoy is *our* culture, even the God we worship is *our* God.

Rules and regulations provide the framework we need to find our place in society without betraying our call.

A community is no healthier than its members.
Rules that pave the way to personal maturity
empower people to give their best;
rules that oppress personal initiative harm us all.

Children engrossed in their favorite television show resist the order that says they must be in bed by nine. Were it up to them, they would stare wide-eyed until midnight. Their "no" to this parental rule may be an expression of independence, but it does not take into account their need for a good night's sleep.

Children express how they feel about these rules, but they still have to obey them. Soon enough they will see that sleep is necessary for everyone, their parents included. Fighting certain rules, proven to be of value to the common good, is as childish as refusing to go to bed.

This is not to deny that certain rules and regulations have curbed human freedom arbitrarily; oppressed people revolt against them in the knowledge that the law ought also to be a liberating force.

The decision to change unjust rules and to replace them with just ones can alter the course of history. This does not imply that rules in general should be abolished, but that their enforcement needs to be fair.

Each of us must discover for ourselves what laws mean in relation to our growth as persons. Do they help or hinder our advance in faith, hope, and love, in social justice, peace, and mercy.

A sign of childishness is that we rebel against rules that do not fit into our notion of what life should be like. Our guide is not reality as it is, with all its limits, but our own fantasy of unfettered freedom.

The rule of law is the best protection of a free country. To obey reasonable laws reasonably lends vigor and conviction to a balanced life of labor and leisure. Time-tested rules *and* regulations are not curtailments of freedom but human and divine directives helping us to know and accept our limits and potentials.

VII.
Knowing My True Self

We hear much about the importance of developing as persons, being who we are, respecting our uniqueness. Are these references to knowing my true self a source of selfishness or a celebration of our call?

ꙮ

Self-centeredness means that people and things have value only if they contribute something to my personal story. I measure their capacity to foster *my* wants, *my* needs, *my* plans.

I may even use the life of the Spirit as a way to focus attention on myself. The goal of prayer is no longer loving surrender to God but the acquisition of graces conducive to the halo of holiness to which I aspire.

At the root of selfishness is a misunderstanding of the true meaning of the word "self." I am not a country unto myself. I need contact with God and others if I hope to be able to celebrate my call.

As long as I approach people in a functional way, as tools to use or things to be manipulated, I fracture my best possibility for emergence.

I need others precisely because they, too, are unique selves. Participation with you in your providential selfhood brings my call to its completion.

Emphasis on "being myself" and "developing as a person" can be helpful on the condition that I live in unselfish openness to the dignity and worth of others.

A truly personal relationship is not easy to attain, especially in the beginning. Inborn egoism, irrational fears, lack of trust are all stubborn obstacles to other-centered love.

In opening up to others as persons, I also risk being hurt. If I have the courage to approach other people unselfishly, I may soon experience a liberating effect on my life and outlook. Even my spiritual life blossoms because of the Divine Love to whom I surrender in confidence. Trust in God's providence becomes a leading theme in my life and an example for others.

Self-emergence is a matter first of living and then of thinking. I cannot think myself into being myself. I can only let myself be.

Reasoning about the mystery of my call is fruitless unless I open myself to the messages God sends me through other people. My true self can unfold only when I accept humbly that life has to be lived in the twilight of partial understanding, not in the clarity of full insight.

If I persist in excessive examination of my defects and failures, I may find myself trapped in introspection and futile attempts to gain insight into why I'm not perfect yet! The more I focus on myself in isolation, the less time and energy I have to discover who I really am.

Self-presence is not the same as self-analysis. To know myself as an effective organizer, to think reflectively about a concrete enterprise, is to see myself as a "managing me," who masters the world.

To know myself as openness to mystery, to be a person of vision, to inspire others, I need to be more than a product of self-analysis. My inner life has to harmonize with my outer life. A creative blend of stillness and commitment wins the day.

Self-emergence is never static. It emits new data. It initiates questions that call for heartfelt responses.

When I accept the pace of graced growth God allows, I realize that any approximation of perfection always happens in imperfect ways.

The quest for self-discovery, if it is authentic, leads neither to selfishness nor selflessness. Granted by grace is the light to see myself as a unique epiphany of the mystery that is at once in me and beyond me. By extension, self-identity or self-love means neither selfless absorption in the unknown nor abandonment of my uniqueness to the imposing will of another. Neither does it compel me to reduce the totality of my being to the image I see in the mirror.

When we ask, "Who am I?" we are not alone. This question is at the root of the mystery of life. As persons in the world, we find ourselves in relation to others. At the same time, we stand before that which is beyond our comprehension.

That is why we feel the need to rediscover our worth in a wealth of human relationships, some special, some routine. That is why we also need to resource ourselves in the ground of our being, in the Infinite Love that embraces us and calls us by name.

> *True self-love shares at every moment*
> *in the love of God and others*
> *that gives us our reason for living.*

We love others as they are, not as we imagine them or, for that matter, ourselves to be. We are united in a greater love which carries us through time to eternity.

The height of our experience of selfhood corresponds to the depth of our surrender to God.

A better word for self-esteem is call-appreciation. We honor in self and others the recognizable yet unrepeatable call bestowed on us at birth by God. It is a mystery that defies definition. At the same time, it is our deepest transcendent identity.

There must be no opposition between outward expression and inward belief. One flows forth from the other in a unity of thought, feeling, and faith.

Our availability to others may exude an aura of charity but this wears thin if caregiving is not an expression of love which flows from the depths of our oneness with God.

Unveiling the mystery of our call continues until the closure of our earthly window. For us who live by the Great Commandment, love of self is not the end point but the portal leading us to a life of love and respect for others and God in whose presence we find peace.

Part Two

The Self and Others

Prologue

*We reach out toward others
in vain because we have
never dared to give ourselves.*

I.
Openness to Others

*In a world that puts self-interest, competitive isola-
tion, and envy high on the scale of values, what
does it mean to be open to others for their own
sake?*

ᔐ

There is nothing wrong with wanting to take care of ourselves
nor occasionally having to stand alone. The problem comes when
we remain aloof, treat others with antipathy, and compete with
everyone in our peer group to better our position.

We act like frightened rabbits fearful of exposing our vulnera-
bility. We retreat to our burrow and miss the blessings openness
can bestow. We need to accept that even our best efforts may be
rebuffed, but the risk is worth taking.

Undue demands or rude impositions may cause others to withdraw from our presence. A sensitive approach, one that says
silently, "I respect you as a person," may mark the hesitant beginning of a new relationship.

Openness acknowledges those times
when life is a closed door.
It takes a lot of trust to let others
walk in our walled off garden.

There is a delicate line between prying into others' lives and listening attentively to what they have to say. To be open to their world, we must be willing to leave behind what is familiar and follow a new road. Such an adventure tests our trust.

On many occasions we may be tempted to crawl back into our shell or to feel that our attempts at encounter have been in vain.

The danger of self-withdrawal is real. In subtle ways we may refuse to face it. Once we convince ourselves that we want nothing else but to be left alone, we can seal off further contact. We escape the effort of reaching out to others by placing upon their shoulders the burden of proof for our lack of concern.

Why do we prefer to be alone? Is it because we are lovers of solitude or because we cannot bear the interference of people who might impose their standards on us or put us in their debt?

We may compel others to be grateful to us for the sacrifices we make on their behalf. Hidden under the pretense of care may be a secret plan to dominate them if we can. This distorted disposition can corrupt our best intentions, and it often does.

Once others feel that some selfish need motivates our show of concern, they may see through the sham of our solicitude. We are not open to them; we only want to use them.

Even if our interest is genuine, we should remember that past experiences of being betrayed may cause others to be distrustful. In most cases their hesitancy may be traced to the fear that they will be hurt again if they risk being caught off guard.

Our openness should be modulated by the patience to bear with another's prudent reserve. This hesitancy might signify a testing period in the slow ripening of a reasonable rhythm of openness and closure, communion and privacy.

To be open is to revere the "otherness" of each person we meet. It is to let them reveal or conceal as much of themselves as they choose since self-exposure in a competitive culture is always a risk.

We have to be open to the fact that some people may shun our show of interest. Others may feign receptivity but not really mean it. They may simply want to sell us their wares.

If we were to isolate ourselves for any of these reasons, we would neither be able to care for others nor cope with their changing moods.

Learning to accept the give-and-take of different relationships calls for a wise balance between self-withholding and self-communication.

Some people may be at ease with my temperament and mannerisms; others are not. Some do not even hear my message because they expect another kind of person to convey it. No matter what I say or do, they balk at being open. Rather than repeat what I said or force the issue, I need to tolerate their delayed response.

In a culture based on envy and competition, it is not easy to engage in the art of encounter within the limits of each situation.

Depending on the circumstances, I may feel more or less together, more or less alone. As I grow in self-acceptance and other-centered love, I may benefit from an intuitive refinement that guides my presence and response to appropriate levels of nearness and distance.

We ought not to disrespect people who wisely maintain a certain reserve. Rather we should follow the Golden Rule, treating others as we would like them to treat us. We never know when we might meet that rare person whose presence to life tunes in with our own desire to be open. This gift is God's to give, ours to receive.

II.
Interest in Others

I want to express interest in others, but I still fear letting myself go. Can this fear be overcome?

↜

Showing interest in others means leaving the safety of our situation to see the world with their eyes. This outgoing disposition, combined with moderation widens our horizon. It may open new perspectives that take us to new places in our relationships. This is how we rise above a climate of suspicion and let go of fear.

When we show concern for others, sharing our situation with them, we may feel insecure; yet out of this shadow may emerge the shining light of encounter.

It is good to be a person of compassion who cares enough to irrigate the desert of our loneliness with the rain of empathy.

Showing interest in people as limited as we are is more selfless than self-seeking. Only through encounters like these may we find ourselves.

By the same token, any pushy behavior on our part may send up warning signals. Evoked is more fear than trust. Others see us as a threat to their integrity. Our show of interest in them seems to be motivated by self-centeredness, and so they turn away.

The pain of failed relationships is often the cause of our fear of becoming involved with others. Like many in our commercial society, we may have been rejected by someone we trusted–an employer, a colleague, a fair weather friend.

Fear of a repeat performance makes us hesitant to leap into another relationship too quickly. Each new overture to trust may warn us not to succumb to the same humiliation.

Fear of involvement may also stem from the conviction that emotional forces should be guarded like buried treasures instead of being lifted into the light and interwoven with the fabric of our life.

If we listen only to the language of fear, we cannot suddenly master the language of love when we encounter receptive and generous people.

If we have suffered from failed relationships, we may come across as cold and detached. Instead of trying to change ourselves overnight, we should seek the source of our shyness and suspicion. Why do we find it difficult to experience peace and joy? Is it because we allow ourselves little or no room to get past our well founded yet numbing fears?

Faith and trust in someone who really seems to understand us may unchain the manacles of fear and free us to love.

Though rejection can make us feel like failures, we need to decide, as the old saying goes, if it is better to have loved and lost than never to have loved at all.

If we are patient and kind in our dealings with others, we may lessen their resistance and diminish their defenses. Despite our best efforts, they may continue to pass us by. True interest becomes more purified when it is tested. By reaching beyond our failures, we neither overwhelm others with excessive affection nor treat them with indifference.

III.
Relationships with Others

Our loving response to others may lead in some cases from meaningful moments of sharing to lasting relationships. Does the interest engendered by such encounters demand of each party instant self-disclosure? How do we cultivate the art of wise and moderate communication?

∽

In the daily stream of cultural contacts and acquaintances, indifference to others is far more common than warm sharing and mutual concern.

Many people cross our path without leaving any personal impression on us. Occasionally, however, one among the many does emerge as "that" person. For some reason, he or she captures our attention. We recognize their face. We know their name. Between us some bonds of respect may begin to form without the expectation of instant self-disclosure.

A personal encounter cannot be commanded at will. It happens spontaneously. Any attempt to force such togetherness is futile. It will only lessen the chance of some trust emerging.

In some cases, personal contact may be limited to a brief meeting; in others, encounters take place with increasing frequency as a more special bond grows between us.

Underlying the gift of mutual respect is an often unspoken pledge to promote one another's dignity and destiny. Friends recognize how different and yet how alike they are. Their trust builds up gradually over the years until they feel free to discuss their needs and hopes, the views they hold, the values they defend, their past history and future plans, without fear of betrayal or manipulation.

Friends respond to one another's serious and playful moods. Even when they need to act on some decision or to put some decision into action, they wait upon one another's pace. Pushing is inappropriate. They prefer to listen to what each has to say.

False friendship lives for the pleasure of the moment; true friendship walks the path for life. False friends demand attention; true friends let one another be. Their friendship is freeing, not binding or imposing. It opens friends to higher values and humanizes their world.

The affinity of friendship is not something under our control; it develops during the course of a lifetime, if God so wills. Friends make no unnecessary demands upon one another's time. Though we may find ourselves spending more time with each other than with anyone else, it is a mutual choice.

Gone is the desire to dominate anyone or to impress them with our cleverness. We care for their welfare. We bless their originality. We celebrate their creativity.

It is as if we hear them calling, "Come and be with me." At the heart of our response to this appeal is a deep respect for every person's well-being. When we fail to answer the call or opt for closure, we may miss the opportunity of a gifted encounter.

*Self-revelation must be
in tune with the trust we share.*

Humility, prudence, and obedience tell us to what degree, if any, we should reveal ourselves to others.

Quiet presence is the opposite of constant clamor or the effort to dissect every word we say in an attempt to please one another all the time.

What destroys respectful encounter is lack of acceptance of the other's limits and gifts. What greater abuse could there be than one which twists desirable means to suit selfish ends?

To beg the people we love to bare their soul is a sign of insecurity. Such pressure is unbearable. It desecrates the sacred right of others to protect their privacy.

It is dangerous to substitute for love the urge to control the other's feelings. Instead we should cultivate the right balance of distance and nearness as the best indicator of genuine intimacy.

When imposition replaces relaxed togetherness, everyone loses. When soul-baring becomes the norm of our relationships, it is likely that selfishness has replaced love. No longer is our presence to one another enlivened by spontaneous concern.

Soul-baring is a form of bribery. Real togetherness creates a climate in which we feel free to reveal ourselves if and when it is proper to do so, without violating our integrity.

Loving encounter is a mutual celebration of self-emergence, not a revelation of unwise dependency needs. It is a rhythm of giving and receiving, not of soul-baring and possible betrayal.

IV.
Distrust of Others

If I have had a series of disappointing experiences during which I came to distrust others, can I learn to trust again?

໑

If distrust has become a continuous disposition of our heart, we may be unable to overcome our fear of what will happen if we trust others as we once did. Treating people functionally seems to be a way of protecting ourselves from possible hurt, certainly a safe way, though one which deadens trust.

The problem of distrust will not be solved until we are willing to face our disappointments and look for the reasons why we have become so distrustful in the first place? Is the problem personal? Is it cultural?

Circumstances may have taught us to be wary of impulsive declarations of trust and to keep others at a safe distance. We look for the flaw in their armor, their Achilles' heel. We think they want to take advantage of us.

Some distrust may be appropriate in a competitive culture where people think nothing of stepping on each other's toes to win every match, but these experiences ought not to color our life as a whole.

Some instances of disappointed trust stand out more clearly in our minds than others. At those moments we may have been dazed emotionally by the hurt inflicted on us, especially when we did not deserve such disrespectful treatment by someone we thought we could trust. We come to the unfortunate conclusion that no one can *ever* be trusted, that in fact, many people are *absolutely* untrustworthy.

Soon our whole field of awareness narrows. We forget that we may have inflicted the same pain on others, that we may have failed them as much as they failed us. We focus only on the fact that we should be loved and respected. We overlook those relationships that do evoke more trust than distrust, more understanding than misunderstanding.

If we are unable to rise above the climate of suspicion characteristic of a competitive society, we may be too quick to blame others for our own imperfections.

No one escapes this tangled web of sinful inclinations. This is why we must pray for forgiveness.

Harmonious coexistence may still be possible in spite of our propensity to put ourselves before God and others. Grace helps us to rise to the challenge of learning to trust again. Soon we may find ourselves asking less for understanding and more for blessed occasions to transcend our own mistakes and start anew.

None of us can escape the pain inevitably accompanying the awareness that life in a sinful world is never fully trustworthy. Such is our condition since the Fall. Ours is a history of human deformation side by side with a saving story of divine transformation.

The possibility of trust may be confounded by the myth that every moment of life should be lived according to the sentimental standards we see in soap operas! They portray us as weaklings searching for perfectly trustworthy parents, friends, and peers, all the while knowing that this goal is impossible to attain.

That the predominant untrustworthiness of humanity should surprise us is a sign of our prideful tendency to deny the limits of the human condition.

Persecution and misunderstanding are more commonplace than we would like to admit. We meet suffering and loneliness under our own roof, to say nothing of seeing it everywhere in the wider world.

Despite our best efforts to the contrary,
we are bound to disappoint others and most of all ourselves.
Our hope for even a minimum of reasonable trust
may be shaken, but it should not be shattered.

The human condition in this and every age is a watershed of weakness and strength, folly and wisdom, dishonesty and integrity. Prudent distrust may even be a sign that everyone, ourselves included, needs redemption at every moment.

We will be better able to bear the pain of disillusion if we realize that life on earth is never free of some deviation from the divine plan. This is a painful admission to make in a culture that prides itself on perfection, but it would be a mistake to try to protect ourselves from disappointment.

Hurtful, untrustworthy exchanges have to be transcended one step at a time. Peace may elude us, but it is better to be realistic than to live in illusion. The truth is, we may meet in our lifetime relatively few people who can be trusted totally.

Provided we maintain a holy and humble vigilance over our hearts, we may find that healthy distrust can be an incentive to resource ourselves in the infinite trust taught to us by Jesus Christ, who took upon himself the scorn of the world and showed us how to love.

V.
Influences by Others

How can I remain myself when my thoughts, words, actions, and feelings seem to be influenced by others to such a degree that they no longer seem to be my own?

⤳

Dependence and independence are not mutually exclusive. When she nurses her baby, a mother gives of herself while becoming more of herself. Neither mother nor child are purely dependent nor purely independent. They are in effect coforming one another uniquely and communally.

Although this exemplary relationship of parent and child lasts for only a short while, its residues influence us throughout our lives.
Our very nature involves giving of ourselves and receiving from others.
Without this mutuality we cannot even speak of personal uniqueness or communal togetherness.

The question of what is mine and what is yours, the distinction between you and me, blurs when we realize how much we accomplish together. Joys and sorrows, delights and defeats, are not experiences we endure alone.

Inwardly and culturally, we speak the language we have learned from others. No matter how inventive we are, a new vision is seldom achieved. Most thinkers express in their own creative way the insights and conclusions of those who have gone before them.

The light which has been shed already on our past invites us to look again at the present and to think about the future. This does not mean that every idea I have must be wildly innovative. This is at best a rare feat since human thoughts are more often repetitive than creative.

Exceptional creativity is a gift granted to a few trailblazers. We share in their gift when we bless their originality and do not envy it. It inspires our own use of hidden talents and highlights secrets ready to be disclosed. To transcend the present moment, we need to consult the original thinkers of great epochs of the past. In our own limited but personal style, we strive to integrate their insights into our emerging plans for the future. This means coming to a deeper appreciation of ourselves in relation to the influences of others so that together we may grow to the fullness of human and spiritual maturity.

Though our thoughts, words, actions, and feelings may be influenced by others, we cannot ask them to bear the burden of responsibility that belongs to us. We confront the agony and ecstasy of our own story when we read of the journey of another's soul.

Authenticity means experiencing life in such a way that we appraise it thoroughly and then decide which direction to pursue in accordance with our current task and the new challenges God places before us.

We are not merely passive receivers. We are acting persons endowed with the limited freedom to choose our own destiny. No matter what influences permeate our environment at the moment, we may reject, modify, or adopt any or all of them with no hint of self betrayal.

Walking on the street or locked in a prison, hale and hearty or deadly ill, we humans retain our nobility and uniqueness. We are free to transcend silently, if not actively, the most inhuman of influences because of our spirit.

We can resist those who persecute us; we can refuse to allow them to enter our world of meaning. We never need to sacrifice our freedom, unless we *choose* to do so.

If this power of choice is denied to us under oppression, the spiritual impact of our suffering may still serve to forestall the sacrifice of freedom in the future.

How vast is the difference between blessed presence to one another and burdensome prejudice! The respect shown to us by loving others creates an inviting climate for the discovery of some hitherto unknown values in ourselves. Prejudice, by contrast, halts personal growth and causes our sense of self-worth to disintegrate.

To acknowledge another's influence does not deny our own uniqueness. It encourages more appreciation. Every disclosure of who we are is an invitation to further growth. Every time we think we have reached the end, we find a new beginning.

VI.
Aversion to Others

Suddenly, seemingly for no reason at all, a feeling of aversion to others may well up in our heart. Why does this happen, especially when we can see much good in them? Should we deal with this feeling openly or push it away?

ᔐ

No two persons possess perfect affinity. Even when we admire others greatly, we may be repelled sooner or later by some sides of their personality. This does not mean that we have changed for the worse; it only signifies that we see others more realistically as they are.

We are all subject to the universal experience of conflict between good and evil within ourselves. While desiring to love others nonjudgmentally, we may feel as if we are being overtaken at times by unreasonable aversions to them. When we least expect it, we may be torn by these conflicting feelings. This experience of disharmony is difficult to accept but so is the futile attempt to repudiate the pain of imperfect relationships.

To attain the unity we desire, we believe falsely that we must repress our not-so-nice feelings. Even modest affinity can only be experienced when we own these feelings, when we are able to listen to what they tell us about ourselves and how we relate to others.

We are not passive victims of uncontrollable passions, but people with likes and dislikes that are often unexplainable.

*By facing even our most
detestable feelings honestly,
we can begin to humanize them.
Even felt repugnance can offer
us a teachable moment.*

I may dislike you because you are inconsiderate, lack good manners, and are prone to put on airs. I may also dislike you because of the tremor in your voice or the way you style your hair. What is important is my willingness to confront these feelings in such a manner that I not judge anything or anyone ultimately because of my personal distaste.

Nothing can be gained by pushing feelings into the background. We should live with them as they are and seek their meaning without allowing any of them to influence us unduly.

Just as I allow myself to feel fear of pain as I trudge to the dentist's office, so, too, I should allow myself to feel aversion while I continue to love. By loving myself and others in spite of our weaknesses and failed affections, we may discover what it really means to care.

Our emotional response to situations and persons is not under direct control of our volition. Often repugnant feelings arise so suddenly we do not even know what in this person repels us.

In regard to the specific aversion we feel to others, we should distinguish between a fundamental contempt for them as human beings and a superficial dislike of certain characteristics they display. Many friendships have been dissolved because one friend became so preoccupied by a petty unpleasantness in the other that all of his or her attractive qualities were overshadowed and forgotten.

To be mesmerized by any one unpleasant trait causes an upsurge of irritation and obscures whatever the virtues others may possess.

Only when I am clearly aware of hostile feelings and their source within my heart can I learn to live with them and not feel compelled to change them overnight.

Reformation takes time. Repugnance can signal its start. Once I arrive at this insight into my own experience, I may smile in retrospect and wonder how I could have been repelled by such a small detail.

If I regret the arousal of aversion and strive strenuously to silence it, I may unwittingly harm my chances to mature. Accepting averse feelings and learning to cope with them gently but firmly is wiser than fighting harshly to dispel them.

When others act ungraciously, I may see in their manners a mirroring of my own pretentiousness. There is true wisdom in the adage that we detest in others what we most abhor in ourselves.

If I am boorish but do not admit to my discourtesy, I may be repelled when vulgar persons manifest publicly what I conceal from my own self-perception. While they arouse guilt and aversion in me, the origin of these feelings–my own secret self-reproach–may remain hidden.

The fire of my antipathy is often kindled by envy and jealousy. People who find these feelings so repulsive that they refuse to recognize them as their own are especially in danger of self-deception. Unless they come to the painful affirmation of their own faults, they will never learn how to face themselves and others frankly.

Feelings of aversion may be related to past experiences. In my early years I may have been embarrassed by my elders. Any anger I expressed evoked scolding, even punishment. So I concealed these feelings, even from myself. Today, meeting someone whose comportment reminds me of those who hurt me may resurrect the hidden anger I still feel. I may dislike such persons immediately and intensely without understanding the source of my sudden repulsion.

By initiating a conversation with my own feelings, I may be able to take a different approach to others. I may come to accept people I used to shun. This is a step beyond merely affirming intellectually that I need to change. It is a step away from repugnance to reconciliation. It is a move beyond aversion to empathy.

VII.
Respect for Others

*What is the basis of respect for others when their
attitudes and actions seem contrary to our personal beliefs?*

⬳

It takes courage and compassion to respect people in general,
but more so when their comportment is different from ours. They
may be convinced that their style of life is the right one for them,
and that they have an obligation to strive after it.

To respect who they are does not mean we have to agree with
what they do. Until they are proven to be wrong, they may be
more worthy of our respect than people who play to the crowd and
pursue their dreams half-heartedly.

*Every person has an innate right
to his or her own honest pursuit of
a life call, a vocation, and an avocation.*

The goals people seek are never too far from the forefront of
their attention. We may disagree with their mission and vision, but
we may not deny their right to pursue them.

In the event that what we want has blinded us to the truth others see, there may be room for sharing of our views.

For this respectful dialogue to succeed, we should not start to question one another's sincerity. Because of our background, education, and personality, we may have missed one or the other opportunity to widen our view.

If we are trapped in outmoded forms rather than open to new ones, we may fail to see what others have already discovered. In this light, it is wise to recall that the original meaning of the word *respect* is "to look again."

In respecting others, I review what they have seen so that I may widen my vision. It is unlikely that we shall ever meet a person whose attitudes and actions are replicas of our own. That is why we should be slow to anger and quick to forgive.

Especially in matters involving practical decisions and preferences, there is always more to learn. The more mindful we are of our own deficiency, the less likely we are to be irritated by the mistakes of others.

Difference and opposition stimulate the search for truth. Such tensions impress upon us the need to respect what we do not yet understand and not to judge lest we be judged. This is the basis for mutual respect.

If I demand that you adhere to my standards rather than exchanging my views with you, I forfeit the opportunity for honest communication and the search for truth.

I must respect you because of your dignity as a human being created in the form and likeness of God. This judgment of value is your due. It is not something forced from me but a privilege I accept.

Compelling myself to be respectful of others because I have been told to do so can be a deadening experience. Lively respect is always rooted in awareness of the other as graced by God.

As Scripture says: "You have heard that it has been said: You shall love your neighbor and hate your enemy; do good to them that hate you; and pray for them that persecute you: that you may be the children of your Father who is in heaven, who makes his sun rise upon the good and bad, and rains upon the just and the unjust" (Matthew 5:43-46).

Some people compound their problems because they fail to realize that "like" and "love" do not mean the same thing. We can *like* only those for whom we have an affinity, but we can *love* those for whom we feel a distinct aversion. We can at least learn to disagree agreeably with them.

While I may not like a person who is bigoted, cruel, or conceited, I need to nurture my respect for their innate dignity in the Divine. While I hate the sin, I must love the sinner. This conviction implies that the root of respect for others is not their behavior but their humanity and its possibility for redemption. In this way, we distinguish between respect for the behavior of others and respect for others as called to find the destiny decreed for them by God.

Only when we break away from automatic reactions of disapproval, disrespect, and condemnation can we begin to live in the respectful presence called for by Christ.

When I find myself rejecting others simply because their values do not coincide with mine, I should question whether or not my own response is true to what I believe. Do I care for others only when they are pleasant, sociable models of my own ideal of respectability? Do I care only for those who confirm my life while I reject those who cause me trouble?

It may be possible for me to listen more respectfully to the communication of others once I admit that I could be wrong.

The meaningfulness of another's journey through life should remind me of our common humanity and arouse more compassion. No one should affirm beliefs alien to their faith since this would betray an illumination of truth they cannot deny.

It requires a high degree of maturity to be able to
perceive candidly what in others repels me
and, at the same time, to respect them
as human beings
seeking to fulfill their potential.

To love people whose ideals are hostile to ours calls for a deepening of the life of prayer. As we grow in presence to the Divine Presence, grace spreads through our life and softens our propensity to judge others ultimately.

In humble presence to the Lamb of God, people appear to us in a new light. This glow does not eradicate the ugliness of sin, but it does enable us to respect ourselves and others as recipients of our Father's loving care.

With the help of grace, we may be able to remove the veils of suspicion that shield us from the truth of our essential goodness. Even though we see ourselves among the weakest and most wounded of God's children, we never despair. His mercy always surpasses our misery.

Part Three

The Self and Community

Prologue

*All around us
is an infinity
into which we flow
together
and live anew*

I.
Community and Freedom

*Is it possible to enjoy freedom
within the confines of community?*

⇌

Our personality profile, our talents and skills, our yet to be disclosed potentials--all show how complex life is and all temper our illusions of unfettered freedom. We learn that our inner life, our call by God, cannot be separated from our situation, our relationships, and our world at large, and that freedom and unfreedom coexist in the same person.

Limitless independence is a futile fantasy. Freedom is always limited. It does not allow us to float above the daily round of facts and obligations, of duty and responsibility.

Life in society demands dependence on one another. We are bound together by our surroundings, our personal history, and the ups and downs of daily life.

Mutual dependence increases as more and more specialists become experts in distinct fields separated from one another. In the past there may have been one general practitioner to care for our health. Now teams of medical experts, nurses, and technicians may be consulted. Teamwork makes us dependent on one another. It is tough to fulfill our calling alone. More and more we rely on an internet of people to assist us.

The notion that freedom unbound by the confines of community would magnify my chances for self-emergence is false. I may never find the true meaning of freedom if I do not embrace my own and others' limits.

Reflection on everyday events reveals the forces of pride, the unbridled passions, which compel us to feed the fantasy of boundless liberty. Human freedom is culture-bound and community-oriented. It teaches us that we can only emerge as free persons when we accept responsibility for our actions and rely on others to help us to bring them to fruition.

When we deny our ties to society and strive to attain a life unimpeded by social concern, we isolate ourselves from the community we need to sustain us. We diminish its full flowering as well as our own.

Willful disregard for social concerns, because they demand more than we seem willing or able to give, is a formula for frustration, lawlessness, and disorder. Rather than showing how community life guarantees personal growth, we judge its call to duty and responsibility as an unfair imposition on our freedom.

Compliance with community is not a cause for defiance. It is a condition for finding and defining who we are. To effect wise decisions, personal freedom must be pursued in a communal setting.

Freedom is more than the right to choose our own destiny or to enforce our beliefs. It is a privilege granted to us in limited proportions by God. It ought not to be abused for any reason.

Freedom is a value to be lived,
not a license to do what we please.

In the company of like-minded others, we do our best to respond to the demands made on us by life in community. What hampers freedom most is to contest the group to which we belong with no sense of concern for the feelings of its members.

In times of transition, a gentle yet firm approach to change is the best way to exercise my freedom. This quest for stability should not spring from selfish whims divorced from reality. It should be a sincere response to my desire to preserve the values I and others cherish and hope to pass on to future generations.

I should strive to help my community to move from restraints and restrictions no longer in tune with the demands of history. Freedom means at this moment to search with others for better means of renewal and revision.

Free will exercised within reasonable limits is the hallmark of our creation. It implies acceptance of the limited presence we are over a lifetime. Because we live on this earth with others, we must not expect our vision to coincide with the course of their life or the span of time granted to any one community.

This is no cause for despair, no reason to reject society. It is an invitation to seek new venues for self-emergence within the confines of community.

Freedom by definition is always situated. Unlike the fantasy of unlimited license, it enables us to live in reality as it is and to discover who we are in openness to the whole and Holy.

II.
Community and Calling

How is my calling in community
related to my personal life and profession?

∽

Professional calling and commitment to community should complement one another. If I identify mainly with the mechanics of daily routine, instead of experiencing myself in relation to higher values, I harm myself and my community. I may seek my worth not in and through my calling to serve but in the status my profession conveys.

The tendency to identify personal value with professional prestige is pernicious. I may have a poor job and still be a fine person. I may also have a fine position and be less of a person.

Security should not be equated with fame nor should self-affirmation rely on reputation. When status becomes my highest value, competition at any cost may rule my life. Insecurity, jealousy, and envy run rampant.

If another employee receives a promotion, I hold it against her. If a co-worker deserves a raise, I tell others I deserve it more. Such selfishness makes living in community a continual struggle to claw one's way to the top.

When position becomes the main criterion of my worth, I may seek work that does not suit my gifts or dispositions. I may want to be a nurse, but since nursing does not rank as high as teaching on the scale set by my family, I may convince myself that the classroom is a more important place to be than the hospital. This forced decision not only lessens my chances for happiness; it also affects those people who may now be served by a mediocre teacher who could have been an excellent nurse.

My choice of profession has to take into account the needs of society. There are times when sacrifices of personal interest must be made to serve the common good.

If I flaunt my commitment to community and aim only for self-enhancement, I am bound to feel some sense of loss, frustration, and lack of fulfillment.

The seeking of status for its own sake is unsatisfactory. It erodes my contact with community and demeans the culture for which I and others bear responsibility.

The finest persons we may ever know may be found in the humblest ranks of society. Farmer or pharmacist, baker or banker, seamstress or stockbroker–whatever we do, the question is: are we giving it our best? If the answer is "yes," then our sense of worth and the way we work will complement one another.

If I am not blessed with an exact fit between what I do and who I am, I can still maintain my serenity. The unfulfilling parts of my position may be more endurable when I know that I do what I do for the sake of a cause and a calling that transcend the limits of family and community.

When I make my best intentions known, when I move with grace from decision to action, I become an agent of transformation at home and in the workplace.

Having good intentions but not acting in accordance with them serves no one. My motivations must be incarnated in good works that help me and others to mature.

When my commitment to community is unrealistic, I cannot expect to achieve perfection in every phase of my calling. Instead of failure becoming an opportunity for renewed creation, it becomes an obstacle.

My profession offers me time and space to come to know myself and how God wants me to be present to the people, events, and things I meet along the way. In due time I sense a bond growing between my social orientation and the Spirit's inspiration.

Only by building upon the communion
that is can I anticipate the communion that is to come.

My life should be a movement toward reconciling service and solitude, labor and leisure, work and worship, even if this means a change of pace and position. The bond between togetherness in community and self-expression in daily activity is a goal to be reached slowly but steadily.

Loving care for husband, wife, and children, dedication to maintaining the sacredness of our home as the basic unit of society, enable us to respect the larger human family to which we all belong.

Daily duty, however ordinary, extends to the whole of humanity. To view our calling in the light of a worldwide community could be likened to the exquisite union of the dancer and the dance.

The tension between success and failure, plenty and want, give way to a graciousness of form and expression dedicated to reconciling each unique service we render with the common ground of our humanity.

We are less likely to become so absorbed in whatever we are doing that we fail to see the connection between this service and the love of God that sustains and transforms every effort we make to build a better world now and for generations to come.

III.
Community and Solitude

*Many different demands pulling at us simultane-
ously add to the clamor of community life. We seldom find time to be alone, yet the need for solitude
persists. How can this tension become less stress-
ful and more creative?*

ᨓ

Living with and for others inclines us to neglect the still small
voice heard within our heart. Solitude is an invitation to rediscover the right balance between the unique and the communal
sides of our life call. This homecoming helps us to be truly present
to ourselves and others.

*In solitude we can listen to revelations of life
that may go unheeded during hours of day by day dedication.*

Present to myself in solitude, more resigned to the slow
unfolding of time, I may enter a world neglected and forgotten in
the aggressive thrust to conquer time.

Solitude is a source of strength, restoring me to myself. When
I rest in solitude, in quiet presence to God's call, I see the world
with eyes of wonder: snowflakes falling, birds singing, dew drop-
ping from sheaves of grass on cool mornings. I feel what it means
to live in my body. I sense in the freshness of each new day the
mystery embracing me and my community.

Awareness of life's meaning, its pristine value, may be lost if I lose myself in the agitation of activism while failing to return to myself in recollection.

Solitude is not a luxury reserved for moments when I am alone. It ought to be a lasting way of life that redeems me from the fragmentation caused by constant distractions.

Solitude returns me to wholeness. It refreshes my sense of service to community. In the midst of people to face and places to go, presence to God, self, and others in solitude may help me to anchor action in contemplation.

The more prone I am to be swept away by activity, the more I need the balancing harmony of solitude. From this place of grace, I can approach my tasks in community relaxed and confident that I am more in tune with what God intends.

Solitude is neither the end
of engagement nor the
cessation of action.
It is a binding of involvement
to its source and inspiration.

If doing becomes the main value in my life, it may deflate my purpose for being. Action then becomes an obstacle to contemplation. I find it difficult to put my heart in what I do. I place myself at risk for the erosion and depletion of social presence.

If I cannot listen to my inner voice in solitude, what makes me think I can pay attention to others? Even when I try to listen, I may only hear halfheartedly. Needs go unnoticed because I am too busy crafting responses to my own agenda.

I cannot empathize with others if I have lost the ease of listening to what God asks of me. I would rather escape life's demands through self-deception or throw myself frantically into work than take time off to be alone with the Alone.

The clamor of constant activity tempts us to live unreflectively, but the need for solitude persists. It is not a luxury for an elite few but a survival measure for all in today's world.

Present in solitude to the whole and Holy changes us for the better. No matter how busy we are, we find ourselves assenting to the warmth of God's love that surrounds us at every moment.

We begin to see our daily tasks as invitations to immerse ourselves in the grand plan of our Divine Guide. Whatever we do has a deeper meaning. We notice that hectic agitation no longer separates us from the hidden messages common endeavors contain. We discover that time is not a collection of moments to be filled but the manifestation of a mystery whose meaning is not ours to master.

IV.
Community and Consensus

Consensus is a feature of life in community. Is it a help or a hindrance to my growth as a person? What if my opinion differs from what everyone else seems to agree upon? Can I learn to disagree agreeably or is compromise the only alternative?

⇦

Consensus in community should be an expression of shared concern, creating room for people to be themselves. If mutual respect is brushed aside or eliminated altogether, consensus gives way to only personal gain. It may then be a hindrance to the emergence of self.

No community can continue without consensus;
neither can it advance when people agree
just to please one another.

Community does not consist of a crowd of conformists unable to make personal decisions. We may consent to a proposal either because we believe it is of perennial value or because it seems to benefit our community at this moment of time. In either case our decision should be inspired by the interests of all concerned beyond anyone's isolated plans and projects.

If we only favor those proposals that suit us personally, if we ridicule those that do not, we may abuse the very concept of community by gathering forces around us that posture consensus.

Adversity is a blessing. It may help us recognize our willful distortion of mutual concerns. Disagreement can refine our thinking and prevent us from pushing for premature closure.

Our efforts to sidetrack legitimate consensus may be rooted in thoughtful reflection but more often than not wounded pride is the culprit. Under the pretense of preserving community ideals, I marshal others to serve my ambitions. My response is not to tolerate mistakes but to push for a position more to my advantage.

Grace may grant me the light to discover that mine is neither a sincere commitment to community nor a willingness to sustain the ideals of its members. All I care about are my own chances for promotion.

The will to power poisons my sense of what a community ought to be. Life becomes a game in which I calculate the moves I make to assure that I receive top billing. I would rather build a false consensus than risk a challenging encounter.

I want pat answers, not fresh proposals. I steer clear of anyone who disagrees with me. I classify them only as a help or a hindrance to my objectives.

Only when we temper the will to power and reaffirm our commitment to serve God and others in humility can we enjoy the warm spontaneity and quiet effectiveness that characterize a Christ-formed community.

Any time the push for consensus represses
our respect for persons in their uniqueness,
it becomes counterproductive.

Silencing legitimate dissent is the preferred tactic of a crowd or a collectivity. Even when strong, outspoken persons act with the best of intentions, they risk the danger of violating the calls and convictions of others, who may follow them in thoughtless adulation.

Cultic groups solicit the adherence of needy people. Even when they do not agree with their leaders, they fear the consequences of crossing them. They find it easier to concede than to confess their misgivings.

The line between cowardice and true consensus is not readily discernible. What we call a concession may be an excuse not to stand up for our convictions.

Though our opinions differ from the current consensus, they are not necessarily invalid. It requires vision and courage to evaluate an agreed upon decision from another perspective, especially when some do not take kindly to our views.

In deciding whether to speak or to remain silent, we should neither be intimidated by disagreement nor enticed by the possibility of gaining prestige in the eyes of people who pride themselves in being on the same page. Our decision should be made in the light of our pledge to maintain integrity and to move in the direction of what is best for our community as a whole.

Not every proposal can be enacted by the members of a community, but the possibility of more dialogue should always be present. If opposing factions are not invited to elucidate their insights, resentment due to unvoiced opinions may make it impossible to reach unanimity.

Dissent obliges us to think independently. It invites us to listen with respect to those who feel differently. We can learn more from them about community problems than we can from people who "yes" us to death because it is the swiftest way to avoid friction.

No matter how insurmountable our differences may seem to be, commitment to community inspires us to transcend the tension of disagreement and arrive at a workable resolution. Approval and agreement, instead of being forced on various factions, will then spring from reverence and respect.

V.
Community and Cooperation

To maintain community calls for cooperation.
Why, then, is it such a difficult goal to reach?

⌒

We share in the mystery of life from the moment of birth to the moment of death. With our first breath we rely on others. Neglect us and we perish. Nourish us and we survive.

From this fundamental togetherness flows the necessity of cooperation. Cooperation is a condition for the possibility of meeting mutual needs. To rely on one another implies a risk, but unless we make this leap of faith, life becomes unlivable.

To collaborate with others calls for a sense of humility. This virtue allows us to distance ourselves from self-preoccupations and prejudices. It helps us to drop the expectation that others will always be responsive to our suggestions. It teaches us to listen to one another and not to turn a deaf ear to any good suggestion.

Mutual listening converts
collision to cooperation.

Cooperation is unfeasible without genuine respect for the opinions and positions others hold. If we are not willing to endure the tensions that may erupt when two or more persons try to get along, we may put a stop to community life before it starts. In the end we must learn the art of cooperating without undue compromise of our own convictions.

A cooperative person is at least implicitly open to all sources of information, and surely to those which concern decisions affecting the community as a whole. Differences of opinion and a variety of insights are par for the course along the path of cooperation.

Diversity may render cooperation between us and others more difficult, but it does not destroy the possibility of our reaching consensus. If we encourage mutual openness prior to decision-making, even those who disagree with our judgment may rest content, mindful that we do respect their point of view. Any coercion on our part may toll the bell for cooperation.

The deeper our involvement in a cause, the less open we may be to discussion about it. Enthusiasm is not bad. However, when people insist that their way is *the* way for everyone, they miss the benefit of realistic critique.

In their efforts to enlist the cooperation of others, they may so highly extol the splendor of their cause that they fail to see all sides of the picture. Blinded by their own oratory, they exaggerate the outcome of this one plan and face bitter disappointment when it fails.

Such an enthusiastic bid for cooperation may cause us to reduce the richness of reality to one glittering promise on which we fixate our attention totally. Fanatical fascination kills relaxed openness to the best course of action for community and culture.

Pressuring others to join us may jeopardize the limited good we may have achieved had we been willing to set aside our dreams and desires and at least listen to others.

Cooperation means more than enlisting their support. It involves hearing what they have to say, even when we disagree.

If cooperation aims at defending and enriching the community at the expense of personal responsibility, it becomes an obstacle to finding ourselves.

Cooperation in tune with all dimensions of reality is more lasting than fast solutions which preserve one viewpoint to the detriment of all others.

We not only have to cooperate with one another; we also have to operate together for the good of all. We may have to settle for a less than perfect solution while we try together to envision a more meaningful future.

Diplomacy is one of the disciplines disposing us to keep the goal of cooperation within reach. This win-win approach calls for wise evaluation of all the relevant input coming from ourselves, others, and the situation entrusted to our care.

We are free to make our choices and decisions, but not by refusing to cooperate with other people. We can never disregard the agreements and disagreements swirling around us.

The wisdom of diplomacy prevails when we realize that it takes a lifetime to begin to know what makes a person or a community really tick.

By not naming ourselves as final judges of any situation, we become co-seekers of truth and justice. We excel in that creative cooperation which makes life in community a joy to behold, a pleasure to live.

VI.
Community and Commodity

In a society oriented toward production, the usefulness of persons and things may prevail over a consideration of human values. Is it possible to overcome the penchant to reduce life and leisure to commodity and utility?

⤳

Ours is an age exploding with new input. The very heavens seem to open up at the bidding of science. Advanced technical know-how carries us along with unparalleled acceleration. A constant barrage of information leaves us breathless.

We may be furthering our world, but are we failing ourselves? In our anxious striving to streamline everyday living, we may exclude the deeper values we humans crave.

Though our interests may extend to a variety of occupations, we should not lose sight of the way each part points to a greater whole.

When we focus only on practical pursuits,
when we reduce the mystery of life to coinage and commodity,
we may be unable to fulfill our calling.

In a consumer society, we may be praised for our work but not permitted to take enough time off. We may be valued more for what we do than for who we are.

To the utilitarian mind, being useful is the most commendable accomplishment. A business man who pleases his boss all day may be too tired to be nice to his wife and children at night. The more pragmatic his outlook becomes, the less time he has to spend with his loved ones.

When self-worth comes to be equated with a useful approach to life, performance may be more important than persons. We feel like ciphers who can be programmed into the company computer.

We treat people well when they do projects efficiently, but we keep other encounters to a minimum. We have no time to waste with trifles like friendly words or visits.

If we see others solely in terms of their service to society, it pains us to watch them resting or reflecting when they could be producing something. When they sense the sting of our accusing eyes upon them, labeling them slothful or disinterested, they feel guilty about enjoying legitimate recreation.

Such disrespectful looks are destructive. They shatter the possibility of cooperation. This disposition may only gain a new foothold when we start to treat one another as dignified persons loved by God, not as tools to be used for a while and then discarded.

When only commodity counts, I may relax for just one reason: to ready myself for renewed productivity. To read, rest, see a good movie, listen to music, or have dinner with friends is out of the question.

When the pressure to produce takes precedence, I may be less effective. Competition as an end in itself kills the joy of functioning in a cooperative spirit. Teamwork gives us more time to devote to our common goals. It brings out the best in all of us.

An artist like Vincent van Gogh perceives beauty in a farmer's shrunken shoes, in an unmade bed in an empty room, in a beggar's cane and cup. We, too, should strive to discover the values waiting to be unveiled in the persons and things that make up our world. The grace of cooperation will not elude us if we are open to it.

VII.
Community and Communication

How can we find a better way to communicate with the members of our community? What must we do to foster exchanges with and without words that bring us to a new plane of understanding?

∽

Human community is a living dialogue of many worlds of meaning. Each of them is a unique manifestation of what we hold in common. Differentiations of thought, feeling, and perception do not destroy community; they are why we came together in the first place.

Variations of style, outlook, and attitude are found in every type of gathering. From an entire culture to a small town, from a country church to a crowded arena, there is no denying our differences. By the same token, we cannot escape our common need to comprehend the ties that bind us together.

Communication in community presupposes that we are willing to enter into one another's world. What certain ideas and actions mean to me may or may not be the same as what they mean to you. These differences are bound up with our experiences.

How does a common situation affect us personally? What accounts for our response? Honest answers to these questions are never easy. Our preconceived agendas often block the way. We may never succeed totally, but we can at least try to speak from the heart.

Communication is the glue that cements a community together. To keep from becoming unglued, we need to fulfill a few basic conditions.

The first is to see the moment of truth when it comes and face it together. The second is to step away from our narrow world of meaning and open ourselves to the possibility of open and honest sharing. The third is to listen uncritically to what we each have to say. The fourth is to never betray confidentiality when it is requested. The fifth is to make the art of communication commonplace and revered by many.

Nothing relieves the pressures of communal living like honest give-and-take. When we fail to create a climate in which confidential communication is the rule, not the exception, our togetherness may be poisoned by unrelieved feelings of frustration.

Fearing rather than fostering confidential communication may force us to compromise some of our best efforts to serve the common good.

Worse than this, a shared sense of continuity, despite any crisis that may emerge, may fail to materialize. The future we foresaw together may be in jeopardy.

Creating a climate of relaxed, confidential communication with others is difficult in a community that lacks discretion. We should value this virtue as one of the main safeguards of the common life.

A lax attitude toward discretion leads to distrust among the members. If no one can be trusted, then no one will confide in anyone. The very basis for communication becomes corroded.

Indiscretion is as harmful to individuals as it is to the community as a whole. What happens if the moment comes when we need to communicate confidentially with a friend or an acquaintance? Can we trust them or has our own indiscretion made us suspect the trustworthiness of others?

Only in a community where an atmosphere
of mutual trust prevails can true communication commence.

Undermining this art and discipline is overindulgence in empty chatter. Gossip is contagious. It may spread to large segments of society, becoming the favored mode of interaction rather than an occasional, if odious, release.

Empty chatter may hide the suspicion that meaning itself is absent in the life of a community. We should neither succumb to this fear nor continue to indulge in idle talk. At least the attempt to communicate will create a better climate in the community and perhaps jumpstart a new search for meaning.

Once the effort to communicate dies in a community, its death as a living organism may not be long in coming. We must rise above the compulsion to chatter about nothing. Though we may speak less, we may communicate more.

This kind of sincerity helps to restore a spirit of communal living and prevents the danger of unhealthy isolation.

A community relies on the integrity of its founders, but it can only blossom to the degree that its members remain open to the steady expansion, correction, and augmentation of their original vision.

Many different spirits keep a community alive over the ages. They share with one another how these pristine insights, with their perennial values, contain treasures of meaning yet to be disclosed.

The lifeblood of a community is its history. Any worthwhile communication presupposes basing future plans on the solid ground of past fulfillment. Only when we place ourselves on the pages of our lived history can we convey our mission and ministry to new members. Then we may uncover seeds of wisdom still waiting to bear fruit.

To prevent new proposals from being rootless, we need to examine them from the point of view of our original purpose. Listening at this level makes us more sensitive to one another's exchanges and increases our effectiveness. Any insight not related to this living memory may betray our founding spirit. Our future depends on its steady and faithful promotion.

The more we sustain the values that drew us together in the first place, the more likely we are to renew our commitment to compassionate encounter. Only a community that educates us to this gift and discipline can expand its powers of communication, bind its members together, and lay the foundations for future harmony.

Increase of understanding in community is partly a gift, partly a discipline. In either case, it has a negative and a positive effect. Negatively, it means distancing ourselves from our own preoccupations and prejudices. Positively, it entails being attentive to whatever draws us together or pulls us further apart.

Paying attention to personal exchanges is especially necessary in a world that relies more and more on impersonal media of communication. Overwhelmed by the mass of words and images bombarding us on all sides, we may miss the blessing of one-on-one encounter.

A sign that this may be happening is that we listen more but absorb less. We dull our sense to what is really worthwhile. Media fatigue becomes a common problem. We no longer quench our thirst for meaning by drinking from the blessing cup of good literature. We turn instead to superficial messengers with little but popular slogans to convey.

Life becomes difficult to bear when communication is no longer a fountain to which we return for refreshment before continuing to devote ourselves to community tasks and other endeavors. Replacing real exchanges is a compulsion to keep up with the latest.

In service of a worthwhile purpose or project, we need to select what to absorb and what to set aside for another day. Wise and disciplined selectivity can be beneficial on the condition that we take the initiative to limit what we allow into the first circle of our attention. By knowing when to avail ourselves of interesting information, we can pass by rivers of words and fill our reservoir with the Word.

Part Four

The Self and Reality

Prologue

The truth
we have to endure
is our present reality
without the justifications
which time may provide.

I.
Response to Reality

*A poet responds to the mystical face of reality, an
engineer to mechanical questions, a philosopher to
the search for truth. What, then, does responding to
reality mean for the average person? Why are our
responses so diverse?*

ꮥ

The narrative of my life contains data from every moment
known to me so far. It is for this reason that my response to reality
differs from yours. Our talents, traits, and accomplishments are
unique. We experience the same givens in different ways.

A famous painting may mean many things to many people.
One beholds in awe its harmony and depth. Another its exquisite
blending of light and dark. Still another the artist's deft precision
and sensitivity to detail.

Although my personal history predisposes me to move toward
certain persons, events, and things and away from others, I remain
free to respond in my own way to whatever blessings or burdens
life bestows.

I may feel more inclined to be quiet and thoughtful than buoy-
ant and gregarious. My greatest joy may come when I saunter
silently along the shore, or when I recline motionlessly in the sun.
However, I have a family to feed, shelter, and clothe. I must work

to earn a living. How else can I meet the demands of life in this productive society?

To be in tune with reality, I must accept my current position and face its conditions as they come. I seek employment to support my family, but I survive as a person because I decide that I shall work to live, not live to work. Even the most absorbing task will not prevent me from recalling with gratitude that I am more than what I do.

As life unfolds before my awed eyes, I try to respond in a relaxed way to the infinite splendor it discloses. Unless I learn to let go a little, my fears, ambitions, and concerns may get the best of me. I may not be able to respond to the challenges life presents; all I do is react to what I cannot control.

An emotional response tells us only so much. We cannot rely on it alone. Reflection on what this feeling means must follow.

Limits are inseparable from a realistic response to life. I can acquire some but not all knowledge. As much as I might like to have eyes in the back of my head, I can only see facing front or else I must turn my whole body around.

Of what use is it to base my life on the pretense that there are no limits to the ways I respond. The only limitless truth of the human condition is that we are totally bound. Our openness to others is always limited. We can do something but not everything.

Commitment to any call includes the willingness to accept the demands it makes upon us: to parenting, to a profession, to any other obligation this promise entails. The quality of our response determines the degree of our success or failure in matters of duty.

A married man assumes responsibility for the growth and sustenance of his family. Love endears him to his wife and children and enables him to face the hardships and rewards of married life. He chose to bear this responsibility when he made his marriage vows. The conditions coincident with married life offer him many chances to live up to his commitment. Response to this vocation as a lifelong challenge to give and receive love is what brings him fulfillment.

Truly committed presence
to our chosen vocation
is the means God uses to help us
to rise above ourselves and become
better persons in the process.

My response to God's call does not escape the burdensome reality of human limitations. No wonder I grow weary with cliches that seem to hide the real meaning of presence to the Sacred. I want to stand before God as a person who exudes trust, not fear, awe, not arrogance, yet I am tempted to abandon my quest. The abyss confronts me and I shrink from it in despair.

If I pursue the "hound of heaven" as I am pursued, I may see the dawning of a new light. This event marks a turning point in my life. My grasp of reality as emerging from its fountainhead in the Divine Forming Mystery pierces through the cave of my purgation with unexpected clarity. If only for a fleeting moment, I feel what it means to let God be God in my life.

II.
Reality and Self-Deception

I may think that I know what is best in a particular situation, but can I be sure this is so? What are the signs that I may be deceiving myself?

⌒

Self-deception is likely to occur when I force life to fit into my view of people, events, and things. My ideas tend to be absolute; I fail to perceive the middle way between two extremes; I am irritated by the mere fact that others disagree with me; I refuse to reevaluate my stance in the light of hitherto unseen divine direction disclosures.

The inclination to consider my view
as the view of reality is a sign
that I am deceiving myself.

A conservationist and a contractor survey a lush forest. Their thoughts settle on a small tract of land before them. One sees the majestic grove of trees as a source of natural beauty. It should be preserved for future generations. According to him this land ought never to have been sold.

The other sees the trees as obstacles which must be removed so that he can begin building his hunting lodge. According to him, clearing this part of the forest for his cabin is more important than preserving the trees.

Both falsify reality by claiming a view of the land that excludes any other explanation. Their failure to recognize nothing but their own perspective is another source of self-deception.

How many times do we antagonize one another by not tolerating the differences between us? We take one frame of reference as the criterion of all possible worth and deny that other positions may also count. We condemn what we do not understand instead of trying to find a means to complement our own one-sidedness.

All of us practice the art of self-deception to some degree. We may view reality through the lens of our antipathy. In this falsifying light, we sketch on the canvas of our imagination the comportment of persons we dislike, making actions of theirs appear malicious when they are really sincere. It is wise to be alert to this propensity and to try to mitigate it when we sense that something is amiss. Saying the right thing at the right time is not an easy art to learn but it is worth the effort.

Life can be as unpredictable as the weather. Just as I'm about to say with certitude that everything is going my way, something unexpected disrupts the plans I've so painstakingly laid.

I need to take these surprises in stride so that I can welcome the unanticipated as I would an engaging stranger. Initial hesitation, caution, and curiosity should give way to relaxed acceptance of what is. I should neither expect too much from nor deny the eventuality of change.

The only thing that does not change is change itself. Quiet acceptance and alert expectation are wise dispositions to cultivate. They keep me in touch with each moment as it reveals itself.

We should never minimize *maybe* situations nor insist only on definitive answers to reality. Life is not a *yes* or *no* proposition. Most of the time it is a maybe situation. Projects that are worthwhile for one person may be useless to another.

Paradoxically, we may reach the height of certainty when we realize that we cannot know for sure whether or not we are deceiving ourselves. We are not mathematical equations; we are mystery. Our life is always changing and changeable, unpredictable in its unfolding.

Reality is not something that we can embrace or dismiss at will; it is the arena in which we live. It is loneliness and confusion, communion and clarity, truth and deception.

Such fluctuations do not mean that we must flounder hopelessly in chaos and confusion. They are invitations to live in the light enkindled by compunction and surrender to God's mercy. In this light, suffering can be transformed by grace into joy. Our awareness of life as gift and of all people as graced sharpens our self-perception. It makes us less inclined to deceive ourselves by distorting reality.

Eyes enlightened by faith see all that is as an expression of the infinite goodness of our Creation. Faith assures us that this mystery can absorb our mistakes and temper any inclination to distort what is given to us by God.

III.
Reality and Emotion

Some tell us that our emotions are guideposts to reality which should be followed; others claim they are dangerous and should be denied. Can these two opinions coexist in the same person? We are called to accept the limited appearance in time and space that we are. To live this reality dynamically, we should respond to the moment by flowing with it, not only intellectually but emotionally.

∽

Emotion, from the Latin *emovere*, refers to a mode of knowledge that moves us in some way to leave the confines of our narrow self to meet the world. Then, by implication, we return to ourselves to experience this world as ours.

In moments charged with emotion, like a family quarrel or a heated debate, we discharge our feelings. We move, as it were, from the deepest core of our being into that place where we argue or defend the validity of our point of view.

To be a person who senses and feels is to *emote* most of the waking hours of my day. What matters is not that I am emotional but that I not become so enslaved to my feelings that I cannot also think and behave reasonably.

Teenagers enraptured by their favorite singers act and react with charged emotions. They behave in extremes, calling a concert out of this world! Awesome! Unreal! To put a lid on their enthusiasm would be wrong. Energetic adolescents have to let go, to scream and shout, to gyrate to the beat. Their feelings can be read like an open book. To regard them as a disease to be cured is, to say the least, utterly unsympathetic.

We are emotional people, not robots routinized by a controlled, computerized society. Effervescent teenagers who love life and are not afraid to say so, may learn gradually to anchor this outflow of emotion in the ground of their maturing personality. Verbose assertions that come and go may give way to sincere expressions of approval. Feelings and thoughts are no longer at odds.

Emotions are not alien, antagonistic movements, escaping our control; they are integral expressions of how we respond to reality. Emotions can be exalting and depressing responses to suffering or illuminating and perplexing responses to love. Both sets of feelings are appropriate.

Mature responses to emotional experiences vary in accordance with the situation. No two persons feel the same way about love; no two respond in like manner to hate.

Balance is not found by pushing ourselves to act on our feelings nor by succumbing to inaction. All we can do is to trust that they tell us something about acceptance or rejection, elation or depression, reverence or aggression.

In this way we deepen our perception of why emotions open doors to self-knowledge. The opposite happens if we see them as forces endangering self-possession and breaking through the barrier of self-control. Our feelings are not confined to airtight compartments. They are an integral part of who we are. When we deny them, we deny ourselves.

Emotions are like ornaments displaying different colors. They reflect feelings like appreciation or depreciation. We may view these displays as forces to control or as mirrors of our spirit.

We fail to see that attunement to emotions cannot be measured on a calculator. Feelings are not like computers that carry out orders impersonally. They interpret the meaning of inner movements as diverse as anxiety and peace of mind. No matter how slight these stirrings may be, they are still important.

True wisdom is to give my emotions their due
without allowing them to overwhelm my life.

Emotions are special signs emerging from my perception of reality. They signal sides of a situation that might otherwise escape my understanding. I can approach a business meeting with the positive feeling that my presentation will be a success, but still the tension in my neck tells me that I am not as confident as I claim. This emotional response may signal me to stay confident but also to be careful. Something about the situation arouses anxiety despite repeated assurances of confidence and control.

Control can carry negative connotations. If it refers to the repression of every emotion, it can be a destructive force which stifles life. However, control can mean that I assume responsibility for my actions and that I allow myself the necessary freedom to gear my responses to what is called for by the situation.

Accepting myself as not yet harmonious forestalls strained efforts to dispel such disharmonious feelings as envy and jealousy. In fact, compelling myself to praise someone who arouses jealousy may be a subtle and unhealthy form of self-punishment. A more balanced approach is to admit that I am somewhat jealous and then to try to transcend this feeling by affirming my own and others' uniqueness.

This approach is more mature than striving to chain like mad dogs the very feelings that can teach me more about who I really am. Altering my approach experientially is more meaningful than overcoming my faults intellectually. Inner honesty leads to a life in tune with what I truly feel. Harmony of life and feeling is a source of gracious living.

The older we grow the more our emotional response to any given situation should be integrated in our overall orientation to reality. When the integration of head and heart, understanding and faith, reason and intuition roots itself in our presence to the Divine and to the sacredness of people, events, and things, we can begin to envision ourselves as emotionally mature.

When all of life, with its humor and sadness, its clarity and mystery, can be lived in relaxed receptivity to the Sacred, it is safe to say that serenity and equanimity have been found. Emotion then enables us to meet others with compassion and to return to ourselves in peace.

IV.
Reality and Resistance

Some people respond well to change; others want everything to stay as it is. How can we come to terms with those who resist change in general and personal changes in us in particular?

ꮯ

Listening to life makes us sensitive to its silent invitation to change and renew our world of reflection and action. Perhaps life is such that it allows us to be faithful to this invitation. It may also happen that change is not possible at present. Then we must be wise enough to live with things as they are and to make the best of them until another opportunity for growth comes along.

A situation where change has occurred suddenly presents a special challenge. It may be impossible, and even self-destructive, to demand too fast and too forcefully that everyone adapt immediately to this transformation, especially when personal or communal history mitigates against it.

> *The wisdom of change is the art of the possible.*
> *It is our task to improve what can be improved,*
> *to change what can and should be changed,*
> *but also to accept what cannot be eliminated.*

When we become anxious, tense, confused, and irritated in attempting to adapt ourselves and others to new perspectives, we should try to relax. Forget about changing for the time being. Cease fighting to figure out in a flash what to do now.

If we accept wholeheartedly that change is inevitable, without dismissing the reality of anyone's personal pace of adaptation, we can live in the best of two worlds. We feel at home with our own personality and its proper pace of change, and we respect others who, because of their history, experience, and temperament, cannot adapt themselves to as fast or as slow a pace as we can.

Respectful spiritual guides do not force their insights upon people not yet ready to receive them. Once we have reached a certain age, we may be able to see more clearly what needs to be changed in our lives and start anew.

We begin by grounding ourselves in the deepest meaning of our life and calling. We then wait upon God's grace to set the pace of our progress.

Wisdom teaches us not to push for change to the point of exhaustion. We bide our time, wait for the moment of truth, and welcome it when it comes.

My response to reality must include the community where I live. Truth is not solely my concern; it includes my listening to what others have to say in the course of any appraisal.

The virtuosity a good musician displays is inseparable from his or her ability to perform in an orchestra with the other players. Then one person's talent is a tribute to everyone's. If the first violinists played as soloists when they should be playing in tune with the orchestra, they would ruin the musical experience conductor and audience anticipate.

No matter how brilliantly players can perform a particular selection, they must yield to the tempo of other members of the symphony and to the pace inspired by their conductor. The orchestra plays in consonance because everyone in it is at once unnoticed and unique. One section carries the other without offending the ear or demanding undue attention from the audience.

Opposition is no cause for defeat. It should stimulate us to reexamine the sincerity of our intentions and the true worth of our goals. If after reasonable self-examination our opinion remains unchanged, we should persist in a firm but gentle way to bring our convictions to fruition. This appreciative stance prepares us to face the obstacles any progress in the life of the spirit always entails.

If we believe that something is of value, we should strive to find the best way to express it. Many times it is not what I say but the way in which I say it that moves others to agreement or disagreement.

If we fly away on the wings of our own enthusiasm, we may fail to consider the feelings of the people we hope to reach. Our self-assured mode of expression may alienate them before they have time to digest our message.

Though the changes we propose are prudent, they may not appeal to others. By pushing for progress we often meet with indifference. By repeated pushing, indifference may give way to opposition. This may harden into resistance, no matter how many masterful arguments favoring change we may formulate.

Taking into account the goals of those who ask for change and those who do not is far wiser than demanding that others see only the wisdom of our position. The virtue we most need at this time is patience. The proper opportunity to make the right suggestions will present itself. We should be ready to make these options clear without giving undue offense to those who see things differently.

Patient presence to reality makes it easier to reconsider our own style and position, to acknowledge its value and deficiency, and to avoid any unnecessary expressions that may repel others.

An autocratic approach offers people little or no chance to participate in a dialogue concerning ways and means to solve a problem.

Perhaps the acceleration of society contributes to the feeling that everything must be done *now* or else the chance to accomplish it will pass us by. Anyone not harassed by the heat and hysteria of the moment knows that we need time to evolve a project and more time to translate it into action

The course of a river cannot be reengineered overnight. Builders of dams are guided by time, skill, patience, and the desire to progress with precision. Each step is drawn and executed with care until the project is complete. It will serve people now and benefit generations to come.

The attitude of the builder of dams should inspire us when we see that change is afoot and commence our quest for needed renewal.

The results of any change can be seen in the lives of those who either benefit or suffer from this innovation. We cannot care only about what pleases us; our concern must include the implications of transition for everyone affected by it.

True innovators do not allow themselves to be caught in the snare of current trends; they lay foundations for a finer future.

V.
Reality and Permanence

If we experience reality as emerging and changing,
how can we believe in the value of permanence?

ᔆ

Life lived as a stale repetition of rigid reactions is no life at all. It is not a place of discovery but a prison of procedure. If I have to hold myself stiff and unbending as a statue to appear prudent and mature, I might as well be a puppet, not a person.

> *To accept and live life*
> *as always evolving*
> *is a courageous endeavor*
> *worthy of encouragement.*

While certain values are lasting, our connection to them may undergo change. A value remains a value only when we live it. If we create a catalog of goods without putting what we believe into motion to bear fruit, we are liable to lose the little ground we have gained.

Thinking about values should not be a subtle escape from committing ourselves to embodying them.

Living values means that we incarnate their richness and substance in our here and now situation. The change implied by this assimilation does not disclose a valueless vacuum. Permanent values are still present, only our relation to them has grown more personal and profound.

For some people life becomes a call to conformity rather than an invitation to discover the sacred principles guiding our world. They spend a lifetime fixing reality to the wall of their own self-image, only to discover in panic that they have not even begun to penetrate the mystery of human emergence.

Life is not meant to stop at a point of perfection. We cannot cease searching for answers, no more than we can stop asking challenging questions.

> *We should be discoverers*
> *of truth whose sense*
> *of value is not clouded by an*
> *isolated and isolating sense of self.*

Some of the directives we discover may be as old as time itself. This does not mean we lack a spirit of innovation. It means that our search for truth is timeless. We may not experience, live, and pass on these guidelines the way our ancestors did, but our toil has not been in vain since we recognize diamonds of beauty, truth, and goodness when we see them.

The impermanence of life gives us pause to reflect on the permanent values that have sustained humanity throughout the ages. Faithful commitment to these truths does not change despite the mysterious mutability of our lives. Beyond the superficial layers of reality, we bore into the depths of that Eternal Love which gathers under its wings every living epiphany.

VI.

Reality and Transcendence

"I'm lonely, but that's life." "I'm not treated as a mature adult but that's the way it is." Situations like these are hard to endure. How do we face them without becoming bitter? How do we rise above misunderstanding and rejection?

⤳

If reality means only a test of endurance of forces beyond our control, we may be doomed to joyless existence. We join hands with the defeatist, who fights for nothing and smugly pities pained humanity.

To regard life in this way is to disregard our need to discover its meaning and value beyond the brief moment in which we appear. Our presence in this world is not a haphazard event. The tender care of the Good Shepherd calls us forth to make our mark in history.

Though the final meaning of any one event may be hidden from us, it is still of infinite worth in the whole scheme of things. It is to this belief that we cling.

We cannot solve the pain of the present by
imagining a future devoid of conflict.
To truly transcend a situation
we must delve more deeply into it.

We learn that pain and pleasure, sorrow and serenity, loss and gain are mutually implicated. We are able in faith to find an opportunity in every obstacle.

If we view life solely from our own perspective rather than from the viewpoint of history as a whole, we may be so overwhelmed by failed plans and projects that we miss the surprises Divine Providence has in store.

Frustrated in our efforts to improve the situation, we may ascribe every failure to the dimwittedness of those who do not share our vision. The anonymous "they" may become an ever present foe.

An urge to discredit proposals and opinions which are not ours may take hold of us, making us embittered, cynical persons unable to praise the inspirations of others. Believing that our fate is sealed, we cease to search for other means of fulfillment.

A fatalistic stand toward what we concede to be our lasting lot may make it impossible to spot the tiny cracks in the walls we raise around us. They tend to block our creativity and stall our sense of venturing beyond the status quo.

At times I may be misunderstood and underrated but paradoxically, the greater the adversity, the greater the opportunity to test my playful ingenuity in transcending an imprisoning situation.

Often, when I feel myself to be in an "impossible" position, I escape the comfort of habit and open myself to new vistas of growth. It becomes clear to me that progress is not a panacea, that overcoming does not exclude pain, and that improvement is never perfection.

Limitations and restrictions in the face of rejection teach me that to err is human and yet to choose to bear responsibility for my mistakes and humbly accept the challenge of my defeats is to be most free.

Wise moderation in the face of rejection is the mark of a truly loving person. We know it is impossible to guarantee that every outcome will be perfect. That is why we can accept a temporary set-back, even a permanent defeat, and not despair because of it.

When a situation cannot be remedied, we see this, too, as a graced event to be taken up without bitterness or resentment. We choose not to let anything overwhelm our relaxed openness to the higher purpose God may have in mind for us.

Transcendence is not the same as acquiescence. The call to serve God and others is not a hobby guaranteeing my own pleasure and glory. It is an option to dedicate my life to doing good. This choice inevitably involves love and, therefore, suffering.

Most solutions to the problems of daily life are transitory, not permanent. Circumstances change, and we must change with them. Temporary solutions may fascinate us for a while, but we soon discover how relative, insufficient, and fluctuating they are.

This realization may remind us in humility to view life and death not as ends in themselves but as preludes to the promise of permanent praise and glory.

VII.
Reality and Equanimity

A certain disquiet seems to hinder our quest for equanimity. How do we both live with and transcend this tension? Can we combine a relaxed presence to reality with a firm resolve to respond to the grace of growing to spiritual maturity?

➳

Just as we are attracted by light, color, and sound, so, too, are we drawn to the immediate appearance and charm of persons, events, and things. At times this surface attraction satisfies us. We enjoy it. It makes us feel relaxed and playful, but often we have the feeling that however interesting these moments may be, they are not enough.

This experience is an invitation beckoning us to go beyond the immediate, sensuous experience of what we can see, hear, taste, touch, or smell to discover the meaning of reality at its deepest center.

When we enter into this depth dimension, the attraction of the immediate neither fades nor disappears. Surface meanings may still appeal to us, but their fascination diminishes as we face ourselves before God.

Tension arises because we experience a tug of war between the functional and the transcendent. It is as if these two dimensions are for the moment mutually exclusive, but they are not. One should be in service of the other.

We should not become so fascinated by functionality that we neglect the hunger in our heart for a true spirituality; neither should we try to probe the mystery of life to such a degree that we lose track of our need to be effective participants in the working places of family and society.

Maintaining presence to the immanent and the transcendent at one and the same time enables us to care for others and to surrender the outcome of whatever we do to a mystery greater than ourselves.

This appreciative abandonment to Divine Providence is what enables us to be saddened by the death of a loved one, but not to despair; to work without guaranteed reward; to welcome hardship without complaint.

A compulsion for cognitive clarity, a refusal to live in the discomfort of the unknown, throws us off balance. Balance suggests a rhythmic movement between apparent opposites: good-evil, like-dislike, success-failure. Aided by a more balanced perception of reality, we can abandon ourselves to the mystery of life when there seems to be no good reason why a tragedy occurs.

Sadly we tend to reject mystery and to accept only what makes sense according to our narrow perception. We are afraid to admit that life is more than a blueprint for success or a statistical study.

We cannot expect to master life by hurling ourselves headlong against whatever threatens to thwart our progress. We must learn to live with whatever Holy Providence sends our way on the bumpy road from birth to death.

Once we open ourselves to life as it is and to the magnificence of its unfolding, we may be able to rise above the often inflexible features of our surroundings. We are more ready to see the value of every good and perfect gift that comes to us from the Father of lights (James 1:17).

The ground on which we base our life is often the distinguishing mark between being a person who lacks resolve or one who is responsive to the grace of becoming spiritually mature.

Sourced in my Divine Origin, I can live in the tension of seeking my destiny and accepting what Wisdom has in store. The one thing I do not do is to dupe myself into believing that I can predict life like a mathematical equation or explain the unexplainable.

What a difference it makes when I journey inward and find myself in relation to all that is instead of being driven only by the seductive snares of worldly success.

Equanimity comes from within; it is not a mask I can take off and put on at will; it is often unrecognizable. Outwardly calm people may be the most excitable, while frantic types may know how to keep their cool.

The balance of human life is not set in steel or stone.
It is a living rhythm that comes from
resourcing myself in the mystery
so as not to lose myself in the mundane.

As I attempt to integrate fresh insights and experiences into the consonant emergence of my character and personality, I open myself to new adventures at once challenging and confusing.

My fidelity to the call to discipleship has to be steady as a rock and flowing as a river. It implies reaching out to others in service and returning to myself in recollection. I need to assimilate inwardly what I have discovered outwardly on my journey.

The movement of life balances itself when we are able to follow the pace of progress set by grace and still be open to new vistas of experience. In time it becomes easier for us to resist the impact of newness and to maintain equanimity in spite of momentary excitation.

When change does overwhelm us, we should learn to read the signs of lessening equanimity and turn inward. We have to recollect our straying interests, feelings, and perceptions until we are ready again to continue the journey.

Misunderstanding the meaning of equanimity may cause us to withdraw from life. Safe in a secure niche, we may acquire the stability of marble, but we cannot avoid the atrophy which accompanies this attitude.

A truly balanced person is not one who is better safe than sorry but one who has found the right rhythm of motion and stillness. Life is ebb and flow, joyful and tragic, honest and deluding. Only when we accept this alternation can we rest in that "peace of God which surpasses all understanding" (Philippians 4:7).

Free formation flow may become second nature to us once we attain the grace of genuine equanimity. We simply accept life as it is, readying ourselves for these blessed periods of relaxed presence and firm resolve.

At the epicenter of human and Christian emergence, we may be granted a sudden glimpse of the graciousness and glory holding body and soul together. Time itself becomes timeless. Our emergent self ceases its restless wandering and comes to rest in the everlasting blessedness of its eternal home.

Recommended Reading

Become Jesus: The Diary of a Soul Touched by God. Trans.
Joop Bekkers, Ed. Adrian van Kaam and Susan Muto.
Pittsburgh, PA: Dorrance Publishing Co., Inc., 1998.

Muto, Susan. *Caring for the Caregiver.* Pittsburgh, PA:
Epiphany Association, 1996.

____. *Celebrating the Single Life: A Spirituality for Single
Persons in Today's World.* Bombay, India: St. Paul's, 1995.

____. *Dear Master, Letters on Spiritual Direction Inspired by
Saint John of the Cross.* Liguori, MO: Liquori Publications,
1999.

____. *Late Have I Loved Thee: The Recovery of Intimacy.* New
York, NY: Crossroad, 1995.

____. *Meditation in Motion.* New York: Doubleday, 1986.

____. *Pathways of Spiritual Living.* Petersham, MA: St. Bede's
Publications, 1997.

____. *Womanspirit: Reclaiming the Deep Feminine in Our
Human Spirituality.* Pittsburgh, PA, Epiphany Books, 2000.

____. *Words of Wisdom for Our World: The Precautions and
Counsels of St. John of the Cross.* Washington, DC: Institute
of Carmelite Studies, 1995.

Muto, Susan and Adrian van Kaam. *Commitment: Key to Christian Maturity*. New York: Paulist Press, 1989.

_____ and Adrian van Kaam. *The Commandments: Ten Ways to a Happy Life and a Healthy Soul*. Ann Arbor: Servant Publications, 1996.

_____. *Divine Guidance: Seeking to Find and Follow the Will of God*. Pittsburgh, PA: Epiphany Books, 1999.

van Kaam, Adrian. *The Art of Existential Counseling*. Denville, NJ: Dimension Books, 1966.

_____. *Dynamics of Spiritual Direction*. Pittsburgh, PA: Epiphany Books, In Press.

_____. *Foundations for Personality Study: An Adrian van Kaam Reader*. Denville, NJ: Dimension Books, 1983.

_____. *The Music of Eternity: Everyday Sounds of Fidelity*. Pittsburgh, PA: Epiphany Books, 2001.

_____. *On Being Involved: The Rhythm of Involvement and Detachment in Human Life*. Denville, NJ: Dimension Books, N.D.

_____. *Religion and Personality*. Pittsburgh PA: Epiphany Association, 1991.

_____. *The Roots of Christian Joy*. Denville, NJ: Dimension Books, 1985.

_____. *Spirituality and the Gentle Life*. Pittsburgh, PA: Epiphany Books, 1994.

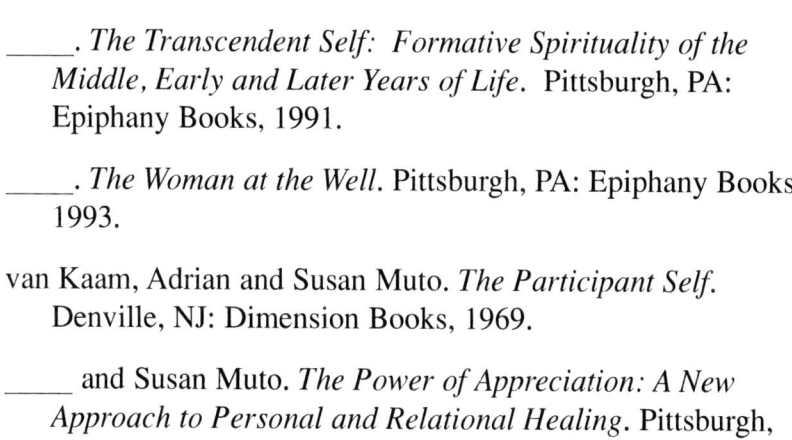

_____. *The Transcendent Self: Formative Spirituality of the Middle, Early and Later Years of Life.* Pittsburgh, PA: Epiphany Books, 1991.

_____. *The Woman at the Well.* Pittsburgh, PA: Epiphany Books, 1993.

van Kaam, Adrian and Susan Muto. *The Participant Self.* Denville, NJ: Dimension Books, 1969.

_____ and Susan Muto. *The Power of Appreciation: A New Approach to Personal and Relational Healing.* Pittsburgh, PA: Epiphany Books, 1999.

About the Authors

Father Adrian van Kaam, C.S.Sp., Ph.D., is the originator of formation science and its underlying, comprehensive formation anthropology. These new disciplines serve his systematic and systemic formation theology. Taken as a whole, all three fields comprise the art and discipline he named "formative spirituality."

He is also co-founder with Doctor Susan Muto of the Epiphany Association, where he continues to write and develop resources in these fields to assist clergy, religious, and laity interested in deepening the life of the spirit.

Father Adrian inaugurated this unique approach in Holland in the 1940's. Upon coming to the United States in 1954, he went to Case Western Reserve University in Cleveland where he received his doctorate in psychology. Shortly thereafter he became an American citizen.

From 1954 to 1963, he taught his original approach to psychology as a human science at Duquesne University. Then in 1963 he co-founded the graduate Institute of Formative Spirituality, received the President's Award for excellence in research, and taught there as a professor in this field until its closing in 1993. He is also the recipient of an honorary Doctor of Christian Letters degree from the Franciscan University of Steubenville, Ohio.

The author of numerous books on spiritual formation, an inspiration to many, a renowned speaker, a prolific poet, Father Adrian's work enjoys worldwide recognition.

Susan Muto, Ph.D., executive director of the Epiphany Association and a native of Pittsburgh, is a renowned speaker, author, and teacher. A single lay woman living her vocation in the world and doing full-time church-related ministry in the Epiphany Association, she has led conferences, seminars, workshops, and institutes throughout the world.

Professor Muto received her Ph.D. in English literature from the University of Pittsburgh, where she specialized in the work of post-Reformation spiritual writers. Beginning in 1966, she served in various administrative positions at the Institute of Formative Spirituality (IFS) at Duquesne University and taught as a full professor in its programs, edited its journals, and served as its director from 1981 to 1988. An expert in literature and spirituality, she continues to teach courses on an adjunct basis at many schools, seminaries, and centers of higher learning. She aims in her teaching to integrate the life of prayer and presence with professional ministry and in-depth formation in the home, the church, and the marketplace. In faithfulness to the principles of the original European Epiphany approach, she addresses her teachings to the contemporary needs of laity, clergy, and religious.

As co-editor of *Epiphany Connexions, Epiphany International,* and *Epiphany Inspirations*, as a frequent contributor to scholarly and popular journals, and as herself the author and co-author of over thirty books, Dr. Muto keeps up to date with the latest developments in her field. In fact, her many books on formative reading of scripture and the masters are considered to be premier introductions to the basic, classical art and discipline of spiritual formation and its systematic, comprehensive, formation theology. She lectures nationally and internationally on the treasured wisdom of the Judeo-Christian faith and formation tradition and on many foundational facets of living human and Christian values in today's world. Professor Muto holds membership in numerous honorary organizations and has received many distinctions for her work, including a Doctor of Humanities degree from King's College in Wilkes Barre, Pennsylvania. Her recently published book, *Deep Into the Thicket*, a series of meditations on *The Spiritual Canticle* is her fifth companion text to *The Collected Works of Saint John of the Cross*. All five books are available through the Epiphany Association at 1-877-EA HOUSE. Proceeds from these publications go to the support of the Epiphany Academy of Formative Spirituality, headquarters for this national and international mission and ministry.